Assessing Internal
Job Candidates

Assessing Internal
Job Candidates

Jean M. Phillips and Stanley M. Gully

Staffing Strategically Series

Society for Human Resource Management | Alexandria, Virginia | USA
www.shrm.org | © 2009

The Society for Human Resource Management (SHRM) is the world's largest association devoted to human resource management. Representing more than 250,000 members in over 140 countries, the Society serves the needs of HR professionals and advances the interests of the HR profession. Founded in 1948, SHRM has more than 575 affiliated chapters within the United States and subsidiary offices in China and India. Visit SHRM Online at www.shrm.org.

Library of Congress Cataloging-in-Publication Data

Phillips, Jean, 1969-
Assessing internal job candidates / Jean M. Phillips, Stanley M. Gully.
    p. cm. — (Staffing strategically series)
Includes bibliographical references and index.
ISBN 978-1-58644-159-3
1. Employee selection. 2. Personnel management. 3. Career development. 4. Executive succession. I. Gully, Stanley Morris. II. Title.
HF5549.5.S38P49 2009
658.3'112—dc22
                    2009030886

10 9 8 7 6 5 4 3 2 1   09-0475

Contents

Introduction

M any organizations consider current employees for open positions before looking to hire from the external labor market. This can be a good strategy because hiring from within helps to motivate and retain employees. Hiring from within can also lead to higher quality hires because the company can assess its current talent better than it can assess a potential employee whose past performance, personality, strengths, and weaknesses are not as well known. However, just because people work for you doesn't guarantee that you fully understand their competencies or automatically know which employee is the best choice for an open position. Knowing what developmental assignments to give an employee also requires a solid understanding of the person's abilities and development needs. Additionally, if a firm wants to emerge from a downsizing stronger and better able to compete, it must know the talents and skill levels of employees to strategically choose who to dismiss and who to work hard to retain.[1]

Internal assessment is the evaluation of current employees for the purposes of training, reassignment, promotion, or dismissal. In addition to evaluating employees' fit with other jobs in the firm, many companies determine which employee skills are needed to execute their business strategies. They then evaluate employees in these skills, and create development opportunities to build these skills in their workforce. In this way, internal assessment enhances strategic workforce capabilities and better aligns employee competencies with the business strategy.

Despite the fact that internal assessment is such a critical staffing function, many companies conduct internal staffing very poorly. Because employees are "known" by their managers and organizations, a common assumption is that we do not need to be systematic or deliberate about promotions or transfers, which can be particularly problematic in smaller firms where most employees regularly work with each other and feel that they know each other's capabilities. This assumption is not true, however, and organizations of all sizes need to think strategically about how they assess employees and staff internally.

In this book, we discuss some of the primary goals of internal assessment, as well as a variety of internal assessment methods. Finally, we discuss two internal assessment models and ways of evaluating the effectiveness of an internal assessment system. After reading this book, you should have a good understanding of the importance of internal assessment and assessing employees for a variety of staffing-related purposes.

Internal Assessment Goals

The primary goal of internal assessment is to identify the employees who will be the best choices in terms of meeting the organization's staffing goals, which usually include high job performance and enhanced business strategy execution. Identifying the job candidates who would be the least optimal choices is also important in informing layoff and downsizing decisions. In fact, removing poor performers can be more important and valuable than identifying good performers.

Table 1 lists several important goals organizations have when assessing internal job candidates.

Table 1. Goals of Internal Assessment

- Maximizing fit
- Assessing accurately
- Maximizing return on investment
- Generating positive stakeholder reactions
- Supporting the firm's talent philosophy and human resource strategy
- Establishing and reinforcing the firm's employer image
- Identifying development needs
- Assessing ethically
- Complying with the law
- Enhancing the firm's strategic capabilities
- Informing downsizing decisions
- Informing restructuring decisions

Maximizing Fit

Why are some very talented people considered bad hires, despite their high skill level? The answer lies in the many ways in which people need to fit within an employment opportunity to be a successful match. One goal of assessment is to maximize the degree to which the person fits the job, workgroup, and organization. We next describe several dimensions of fit.[2]

Person-Job Fit. Person-job fit is the fit between a person's abilities and the demands of the job, as well as the fit between a person's desires and motivations and the attributes and rewards of a job.[3] Effective staffing enhances the degree to which an employee meets a job's requirements—and the degree to which the job meets the individual's needs.[4] Because the most important staffing outcome is usually the employee's job performance, person-job fit is the primary focus of most staffing efforts. From the organization's perspective, if it has an opening for a production supervisor and the new hire is not an effective supervisor, then the staffing effort cannot be considered successful, regardless of how many other positive staffing outcomes are achieved. In organizations that are growing rapidly, the scope of any job expands quickly. To prepare for this, Google tries to hire people who are "overqualified" for the position they are being recruited for, who can handle expanding job duties, and who are likely to be promoted multiple times.[5]

From the employee's perspective, if the new job does not meet his or her financial, career, lifestyle, and other needs, then the match also is not ideal. An individual motivated by commissions and individual performance-based pay is not likely to be a good fit with a job based on teamwork and group rewards. Similarly, an individual who does not enjoy working with people should not be promoted to a supervisory position. It is not only important to consider the fit between an individual's talents and the job requirements, but also the fit between an individual's motivations and the rewards offered by the job. Research suggests that successful person-job fit leads to higher job performance, satisfaction, organizational commitment, and intent to stay with the company.[6]

Just as new hires need to be able to perform the jobs for which they are hired, employees need to perform their new jobs and effectively work with their new supervisors and co-workers. Due to union contracts or company policy, some organizations tend to promote employees because of seniority rather than because they would be the best fit with the open job. Although experience and seniority tend to be somewhat related to job performance, the relationship is not always strong and there is no guarantee that the most senior employees are the most qualified or appropriate for the position.[7] Accordingly, relying solely on criteria unrelated to the job at hand, such as seniority for staffing decisions, often does not lead to optimal person-job fit.

Person-Group Fit. In addition to the fit between the recruit and the nature of the work, the fit between the recruit and his or her potential work team and supervisor is important. Person-group fit (or person-team fit) is the match between an individual and his or her workgroup, including the supervisor. Good person-group fit means that an individual fits with the goals, work styles, and skills of co-workers. Person-group fit recognizes that, in many jobs, interpersonal interactions with group members and teammates are important in accomplishing the work. Employees must be able to work effectively with their workgroup or teammates. Person-group fit leads to improved job satisfaction, organizational commitment, and intent to stay with the company.[8]

Because teamwork, communication, and interpersonal competencies can be as critical to team performance as team members' ability to perform core job duties, person-group fit can be particularly important when hiring for team-oriented work environments.[9] At Men's Wearhouse, CEO George Zimmer rewards team selling because shoppers want to have a positive total store experience. The company takes team selling so seriously that it even terminated one of its most successful salespeople because he focused only on his own sales figures. After firing the salesperson, the store's total sales volume increased significantly.[10] Individual characteristics such as personal goals that are consistent with those of the group, and skills that complement those of the rest of the members, are particularly important to assess in environments in which work is done in groups.

Person-Organization Fit. Person-organization fit is the fit between an individual's values, beliefs, and personality, and the values, norms, and culture of the organization.[11] The strength of this fit influences important organizational outcomes, including job performance, retention, job satisfaction, and organizational commitment.[12] Some organizational values and norms important for person-organization fit include integrity, fairness, work ethic, competitiveness, cooperativeness, and compassion for fellow employees and customers.

Research has found that person-organization fit has a strong positive relationship with job satisfaction, organizational commitment, and intent to stay with the company, and has a moderate impact on employee attitudes and citizenship behaviors such as helping others or talking positively about the firm.[13] It also has a modest impact on turnover and tenure, but little to no impact on meeting job requirements.[14] Despite the potential overlap between person-job and person-organization fit, research suggests that people may experience differing degrees of fit with the job and with the organization.[15] If you imagine someone who is a great salesperson but who does not enjoy working for a particular employer, you can see how people can fit well with their job but not with their company.

How can person-organization fit be maximized? One good way is to identify those qualifications, competencies, and traits that relate to the organization's strategy, values, and processes. Individuals whose work styles are inconsistent with the organization's culture, business strategy, and work processes are not likely to be as successful as individuals who are good fits in these ways. For example, even if Juan is technically well qualified as a biomedical researcher, if he avoids risk, is indecisive, and tends to ruminate over a decision, he may be unsuccessful in an innovative, fast-paced, and forward-looking organization. This may be enough to let him go, especially if the firm is downsizing.

A new hire, including someone moved or promoted to a new role, must be able and willing to adapt to the company by learning, negotiating, enacting, and maintaining the behaviors appropriate to the work environment.[16] To successfully adapt, employees must be open-minded, have sufficient information about organizational expectations and standards (and their own performance in light of those standards), and the ability to learn new behaviors and habits (e.g., low anxiety, high self-esteem, good time and stress management skills, no conflicting external obligations, etc.).

It is important to note that hiring for any type of fit does not mean hiring or promoting those with whom we are most comfortable, which can lead to dysfunctional stereotyping and discriminating against people different from ourselves. One company that evaluates and selects employees based on their fit with the organization and its core values is Johnson & Johnson (J&J). J&J's credo[17] clearly spells out its values: customer well-being, employee well-being, community well-being, and shareholder well-being, in that order. J&J recruits, hires, and evaluates employees against its credo, which is central to its organizational culture. Ralph Larsen, J&J's chairman and CEO, attributes the majority of J&J's success to its core values.[18]

To maximize person-organization fit, determine employees' qualifications, styles, and values that relate to the organization's strategy, values, and processes. Individuals whose values and work styles are inconsistent with the organization's culture and processes are not likely to be as successful as individuals who are good fits in this way. As people move up the company's hierarchy, they are increasingly responsible for shaping and reinforcing the company's culture. Ensuring that the people who are promoted will reinforce rather than undermine important organizational values can be an important internal assessment goal. At the same time, it is not always best for the next generation of managers to maintain the status quo of the company culture. Leadership, innovation, and competitive reassessment all determine what a firm will need in the future.

Person-Vocation Fit. Person-vocation fit is the fit between a person's interests, abilities, values, and personality, and his or her chosen occupation, regardless of the person's employer.[19] Worker adjustment and satisfaction are greater when their occupational environment meets their needs. For example, a social individual who dislikes detail work and working with numbers would be a poor fit with the accounting vocation.

Although individuals usually choose a vocation long before applying to an organization, understanding person-vocation fit can still be useful in internal assessment. Companies that would like to develop their own future leaders, or smaller organizations that need employees to fill more than one role, may be able to use employees' vocational interests in determining whether or not they would be a good fit with the organization's future needs. Retaining valued employees might be easier if an organization can match their interests with a variety of career opportunities within the company. Some people pursue two or more different vocations over the course of their careers because they have diverse interests or because they become bored working in the same career for a long period. Organizations may better retain these valued career changers by understanding their vocational preferences and designing career tracks or career changes for them that place them in new roles in the organization over time that are consistent with their vocational interests and aptitudes. If successful, valued employees who would otherwise be likely to leave the organization to pursue a different type of vocation may be able to pursue multiple vocations without leaving the company.

Table 2 summarizes these four different types of fit.

Table 2. Dimensions of Fit

Type of Fit	Possible Dimensions of Fit
• **Person-Job Fit:** the potential of an individual to meet the needs of a particular job and the potential of the job to meet the needs of the individual	• Intelligence • Job-related skills and competencies • Job knowledge • Previous experience • Personality related to performing job tasks
• **Person-Group Fit:** the match between individuals and their workgroups, including their supervisors	• Teamwork skills • Expertise relative to other team members • Conflict-management style • Preference for team-based work • Communication skills • Personality related to working well with others
• **Person-Organization Fit:** the fit between an individual's values, beliefs, and personality, and the values, norms, and culture of the organization	• Alignment between personal motivations and organizational purpose • Values • Goals
• **Person-Vocation Fit:** the fit between an individual's interests, abilities, values, and personality, and his or her occupation	• Aptitudes • Interests • Personal values • Long-term goals

Complementary and Supplementary Fit. There are two ways people can fit in to an organization or workgroup: complementary and supplementary fit.[20] Complementary fit is when a person adds something that is missing in the organization or workgroup by being different from the others, typically by having different skills or expertise.[21] A research and development organization seeks complementary fit, for example, when it seeks scientists with new backgrounds and skills to work with existing scientists to develop a new line of products. As J.J. Allaire, founder, chairman, and executive VP of Products at Allaire Corporation, said, "It's tempting not to hire people who compensate for your weaknesses—because you don't want to admit that you have any. But... you've got to understand the strengths and weaknesses of your entire group and hire accordingly."[22]

Supplementary fit is when a person has characteristics that are similar to those that already exist in the organization or workgroup.[23] Supplementary fit can be important when a firm needs to replace a departing assistant manager with another person who can perform the job similarly to the other assistant managers. In this case, the organization wants to hire assistant managers with similar skills and characteristics.

Complementary and supplementary fits are relevant internal assessment goals. An employee being transferred or promoted needs to complement or extend the competencies of his or her new workgroup. Together, complementary and supplementary fit help to ensure that promoted or transferred employees will fit in with their new workgroup and bring new skills and perspectives that will enhance the workgroup's and organization's performance.

Evaluating Employees' Fit with Other Jobs. Gauging employees' competencies to determine their fit with the requirements of other jobs in the company is one of the most common uses of internal assessment. When an employee wants to be considered for another position or for a promotion, he or she is typically evaluated against company values and the requirements for the position, and compared with other applicants. For example, when evaluating store employees for promotion opportunities, discount retailer Costco evaluates employees on their intelligence, people skills, and merchandising savvy.[24] Internal leadership assessments can also be used to identify a potential future leadership shortage.

Assessing Accurately

Internal assessment systems must also be valid and accurately identify the candidates who would be the most and least successful in the open job. No assessment system is perfect, but more valid assessment systems do a better job than less valid ones of identifying both the most and least desirable hires from the pool of job candidates. High validity, or accurately predicting job performance and other important criteria such as tenure and promotability, is a critical goal of both internal and external assessment systems. A primary goal of both internal and external assessment systems is to generate high numbers of true-positive and true-negative hiring outcomes, and minimize the numbers of false-positive and false-negative outcomes.

Think about the possible outcomes of an assessment effort. Candidates are either hired or not hired, and would be either good performers or poor performers on the job. As shown in Figure 1, hiring people who become good performers generates the desirable outcome of true positives. Not hiring people who would have been poor performers produces true negatives, which is also a desirable hiring outcome. Both of these outcomes reflect assessment accuracy and are critical goals of the internal assessment effort. The two possible undesirable outcomes are not hiring people who would have been good performers, or false negatives, or hiring people who perform poorly, generating false positives. No assessment system is perfect, but more valid assessment systems do a better job than less valid ones of identifying both the most and least desirable hires from the pool of job candidates and generating high numbers of true-positive and true-negative hiring outcomes.

In some jobs, one type of error can be more important than the other type. For example, because they result in hiring someone unable to do the job, false positives are particularly expensive for high-risk positions such as pilots or surgeons. False negatives, on the other hand, are particularly costly in highly competitive jobs or markets in which losing someone good to a competitor not only weakens a firm's market position but considerably strengthens its competition's market position. When you fail to hire a top scientist, who then chooses to join a competitor, not only does your company not acquire the top talent, your competitor is strengthened. False negatives can also be expensive when a member of a protected class is not hired, sues, and wins a big settlement. The wider the spread of talent in an applicant pool, the greater the pressure on the assessment system to weed out the bad fits and identify the good ones.

Figure 1. Possible Assessment Outcomes

	Poor Performer	Good Performer
Hired	False Positive 🙁	True Positive 🙂
Not Hired	True Negative 🙂	False Negative 🙁

Maximizing Return on Investment

Another important goal is maximizing the firm's return on its investment in the internal assessment system. The greater the return on the investment (ROI) in an assessment method, the greater the assessment method's value. One assessment method may be slightly superior to another in identifying the best candidates, but if its cost exceeds the gain to the organization of hiring these slightly better candidates, then the other method may be the better choice.

Although staffing should always be viewed as an investment rather than a cost, cost is still important if a firm has limited resources to invest. Some companies simply do not have the money to invest in systems that are more expensive, even if they are more accurate at identifying the best new hires and would generate a meaningful return on investment. Sometimes less costly selection procedures (e.g., using better performance reviews and assessments of rotating assignments versus a three-day managerial assessment center) that yield comparable predictive validities can be found.

Retaining top performers improves the return on investment of any assessment system. The longer good performers stay with your company, the greater the return on the company's investment in hiring them. Avoiding bad hires contributes to ROI because bad hires can actually cost your organization money in terms of lost business and underperformance. The return on investment from a new assessment method is the sum of the value of improved performance and the savings from avoiding bad hires over the time the new hires are employed with the company.

Generating Positive Stakeholder Reactions

Meeting the needs of different stakeholders in the staffing process is another assessment goal. As with external assessment methods, if an internal assessment method does not also meet the needs of employees, hiring managers, and recruiters, it is not as effective as it could be. For example, due to the time involved, it may prove difficult to require managers to regularly determine each employee's promotion potential and development needs. If they perceive them to be unfair, employees may react negatively to the processes used to determine who gets a promotion. An assessment method's fairness, ease of use, speed, and ability to predict important job success outcomes all influence whether recruiters, supervisors, and managers use it correctly and consistently. Training in the use of the technique and its benefits, assessing and rewarding people for using it correctly and consistently, and having a reliable and competent assessment-system expert available to help can increase the adoption and the correct and consistent use of new assessment methods.

After spending the time and money to hire, train, and develop subordinates, some managers do not want their best employees transferred out of their unit. This desire to keep top talent for themselves can reduce line managers' willingness to participate in internal assessment programs that could lead to the loss of key staff. If managers fear that their resources could be poached from within, policies and procedures such as a minimum period of time an employee must stay in a job before being promoted can be implemented.[25] Managers should also view talent as a company rather than a personal resource and be assessed and rewarded for their ability to develop talent that is promoted to other areas of the firm. Managers who are known for their development of direct reports, and who are more rapidly promoted within the firm, are also likely to be managers who have little difficulty getting employees to want to be assigned to work for them. Employees may also be required to stay in a job a minimum period of time to demonstrate competence and to discourage job-hopping.

An additional type of stakeholder reaction concerns employees who are turned down for the promotions or lateral moves for which they were considered. These employees may be less motivated or even try to leave the organization. This potential is even greater for employees turned down multiple times for other positions. It is important to treat these employees with a great deal of respect and to maximize their procedural and interactional justice perceptions. Honest communication about what they could do to be more competitive for the position they are interested in—and developing an action plan to give them training or developmental experiences that would better prepare them for the position—can enhance their motivation. If an employee is interested in a position that the firm feels he or she will not likely ever get, it is important to communicate this honestly yet sensitively to the employee. Even better, try to find another career path in which they are likely to be more successful. If a talented employee who has been passed over for promotion or transfer in the past is a finalist for a current position, it can be a good idea to consider this when choosing whom to promote or transfer. The choice may be between promoting the person and losing him or her to a competitor.

Supporting the Firm's Talent Philosophy and Human Resource (HR) Strategy

Another goal of an assessment system is to support the organization's talent philosophy and HR strategy. Viewing employees as investors might stimulate a company to incorporate more developmental feedback into the assessment process to allow the candidate the opportunity to improve his or her competitiveness for a promotion. A firm viewing employees as assets may focus on employee assessment and minimize feedback to employees about what the firm perceives as their strengths and weaknesses. An organization that wants people to contribute over long-term careers needs to view employees in terms of their long-term career potential within the company, and help employees identify and pursue career paths that interest them. In this case, identifying the competencies, styles, and traits required for career advancement within the company is also relevant.

Establishing and Reinforcing the Firm's Employer Image

Maintaining an organization's employer image is an important staffing goal. To establish and maintain its image as an employer, a company must "walk the walk" and genuinely be what it claims to be. An organization claiming to provide an environment where employees can grow their careers will not be successful in establishing or maintaining that image if it does not give employees performance feedback and career development opportunities. One of the goals of the internal assessment process should be to reinforce the organization's desired image among employees. This can also help improve employee retention by reminding employees of the company's value proposition, and by clarifying how employees fit into the company's strategy and future direction.

Identifying Development Needs

Internal assessment can identify employees' strengths and development needs in their current jobs. If an employee's assessment shows that he or she lacks critical skills that will be needed in the near future, training and development can be provided to ensure that the skills are in place when they are needed. Some assessment methods even identify an employee's preferred learning style, which can decrease training time, improve training effectiveness, and increase retention.[26]

Wyeth Pharmaceuticals engages in continuous process improvement, including regular employee skill assessments. Employees failing to obtain scores of at least 90 percent must immediately remediate their skill gaps, which are verified through another round of testing.[27]

Assessing Ethically

Ethics are an important issue in staffing, and particularly in assessment. The entire selection process needs to be conducted and managed ethically, including honestly explaining how test results will be used and how candidates' privacy will be protected, and communicating with candidates when promised. Firms need to think through the ethics of using assessment methods that employees find invasive, including integrity tests. The people administering an assessment need to be properly trained and appropriately qualified, and employees' privacy needs to be protected at all times.

An additional ethical issue involving privacy concerns the confidentiality of an employee's application for another position in the company. If a supervisor or workgroup thinks that an employee is likely to leave, they may treat the employee differently and invest less in his or her future development. Some employees do not want their supervisors or co-workers to know that they are considering other opportunities, even if the other opportunities are elsewhere in the company. It is important to have policies and procedures in place that either respect the wishes of employees wanting to be considered confidentially for other positions or that support communication with the applicant's manager, depending on the company's culture.

Complying with the Law

When it comes to assessment, legal issues loom large, and companies have good reason to protect themselves against potential charges of hiring discrimination. In addition to the negative publicity generated by a lawsuit, plaintiffs are often successful and court awards regularly run into the hundreds of thousands of dollars. One landmark case in this area is *Griggs v. Duke Power Company.*[28] In this case, the Supreme Court found that, under Title VII of the Civil Rights Act of 1964, if an employment test disparately impacts ethnic minority groups, the firm must demonstrate that the test is "reasonably related" to the job for which the test is required. Credit checks, background checks, and cognitive ability tests are among the assessment methods most likely to result in disparate impact.

Monitoring equal employment opportunity (EEO) statistics based on positions and levels in the company is an important part of EEO compliance. The legal liability risk is often greater with internal (versus external) assessment and staffing, particularly when it comes to separation decisions and "glass ceiling" problems that limit the advancement of women and minorities. Companies including Texaco and Coca-Cola have found themselves in legal trouble for promoting minorities at lower rates than Caucasians. *Roberts v. Texaco*[29] found that African Americans were significantly underrepresented in high-level management jobs, and that Caucasian employees were promoted more frequently and at far higher rates for comparable positions within Texaco. A lawsuit lost by Coca-Cola[30] alleged that its written and unwritten policies and practices allowed supervisors to essentially handpick candidates through word of mouth for available positions and to make promotion decisions on the basis of subjective criteria. Jobs were filled without being posted, candidates were chosen in advance, and supervisors disregarded the results of panel interviews and manipulated scores in order to ensure that their favorites were chosen. Because this system prevented qualified African Americans from competing equally for positions, or from even knowing that they were available, they were denied the opportunity to advance to the same level and at the same rate as equally qualified Caucasian employees. This Coca-Cola example illustrates the importance of not only having accurate (or valid) assessments, but ensuring that they are used in a consistent, objective way in making hiring decisions.

Unions generally prefer for promotions to be based on seniority, although it is often possible to negotiate contract provisions making seniority only one factor in the evaluation process. Any internal assessment or internal staffing terms included in a union contract must be complied with. The National Labor Relations Act of 1935 (NLRA) protects employees from discrimination based on their involvement in a union, and prohibits employers from making staffing decisions to discourage union membership. Employees also may not be discriminated against because they filed charges or gave testimony under the NLRA. Although America is rapidly losing its manufacturing companies, unions remain strong in academia, hospitals and the public sector. Internal selection is different in such firms and heavily influenced by union contracts.

Uniform Guidelines on Employee Selection Procedures. In 1978, the need for a consistent set of principles on the use of tests and other assessment and selection procedures prompted the Equal Employment Opportunity Commission (EEOC), the Civil Service Commission, the Department of Labor (DOL), and the Department of Justice to jointly adopt the Uniform Guidelines on Employee Selection Procedures (UGESP). The entire UGESP are available online at www.dol.gov/dol/allcfr/Title_41/Part_60-3/toc.htm. Staffing specialists should develop a thorough knowledge of this document.

The UGESP assist organizations in complying with requirements of federal law prohibiting race, color, religion, sex, and national origin discrimination in hiring practices by providing a framework for determining the proper use of tests and other assessment procedures. Under Title VII, the UGESP apply to the federal government with regard to federal employment, to most private employers with at least 15 employees for 20 weeks or more a calendar year, to most labor organizations, apprenticeship committees, and employment agencies, and to state and local governments with at least 15 employees. Through Executive Order 11246, they also apply to federal government contractors and subcontractors.[31]

Here are some sample guidelines:[32]

- A test of knowledge and abilities may be used if it measures a representative sample of knowledge, skills, or abilities that are necessary to performance of the job and are operationally defined.

- Knowledge must be defined in terms of behavior, and every instance of "knowledge" must be part of a body of learned information that is actually used in and necessary for required, observable job behaviors.

- Abilities must be defined in terms of observable aspects of job behavior, and every instance of "ability" should be necessary for the performance of important work behaviors. Any selection procedure measuring ability should closely approximate an observable work behavior.

- To the extent that the setting and manner of the administration of the selection procedure fail to resemble the work situation, the less likely it is that the selection procedure is content-valid, and the greater the need for other validity evidence.

The Principles for the Validation and Use of Personnel Selection Procedures (available online at http://siop.org/_Principles/principlesdefault.aspx) and the *Standards for Educational and Psychological Testing* (available online at www.apa.org/science/standards.html) are other important resources that provide standards and guidelines for developing and using various assessment methods.

Fair, Consistent, and Objective Assessments. Good hiring practices compare all candidates using the same fair, consistent, and objective information predictive of job success. A false or contradictory reason given for not hiring someone can be considered a pretext for discrimination. For example, if an employer states that an employee was not promoted because of insufficient experience, but the successful candidate has less experience, the contradiction can be interpreted as a pretext for discrimination.

One employment-law expert advises companies to drop the use of vague terms such as "best fit" when documenting why someone was hired or promoted because the ambiguity makes it more difficult to reconstruct the selection process and explain why the candidate was chosen.[33] Recruiters and hiring managers should be able to articulate objective, neutral reasons for rejecting or hiring anyone. The required qualifications must make sense to the EEOC and its state-level equivalents who are looking for a simple, fair process that treats all applicants the same.

Consistently applied, objective assessment methods based on bona fide occupational qualifications required for job performance and derived from a job analysis are best for legal compliance. Subjective assessment criteria that involve speculation about customer preferences or how a candidate is likely to perform on the job are not advisable. Although it is not illegal to reject someone based on subjective evaluations and speculation, subjective evaluations and speculation are precursors to stereotyping, and rejecting candidates based on stereotypes can quickly get employers into legal trouble.[34]

Enhancing the Firm's Strategic Capabilities

Aligning a firm's talent with its vision, goals, and business strategy positions the firm to effectively compete and win in the marketplace.[35] To be able to plan and prepare for future business needs, current talent needs to be assessed in light of current performance, required future capabilities, and employees' potential and willingness to learn.[36] In addition, a company cannot know which employees are good fits for other positions, or what training to offer employees, unless it first determines their strengths and limitations. Although this is true for all companies, it is particularly true for firms changing their business strategies or pursuing a different competitive advantage.

When Federal Express (FedEx) wanted to adjust its policies- and procedures-driven organizational culture to focus on leadership and "getting the job done," it first needed to assess and develop the leadership skills of its mid-level managers. To do this, it used a web-based tool to assess and develop the seven leadership competencies FedEx considers essential for mid-level managers.[37] When a market leader in the food industry wanted to better execute its growth strategy, it shifted its focus from managing costs to generating top-line growth. It recognized that it needed to add new capabilities, including innovation, strategic thinking, and a strong customer focus. To identify where the talent existed, to meet emerging leadership needs, and to develop future leaders in these new capabilities, it conducted an internal talent assessment by presenting future-oriented simulations in an assessment center. Development planning and coaching enhanced participants' capabilities and improved the company's ability to execute its new strategy.[38]

Poor or marginal performers assessed as low potential are typically transitioned out of the company; blocked performers are assisted in improving their performance; and high-potential employees are identified for further development and prepared for advancement opportunities.[39] After completing a strategic staffing plan, one company's information services function (that previously promoted employees based solely on past performance) began considering future required competencies as well. As a result, some previously high-performing employees were asked to leave because they were judged unable to learn and apply new technology. Other employees whose current performance was not high were kept because their skills and experience were consistent with future talent requirements.[40]

Informing Downsizing Decisions

In addition to bringing in new employees and moving employees into other jobs in the company, staffing sometimes involves transitioning employees out of the company through downsizing. Firms often downsize to reduce headcount and corresponding labor costs, or to improve efficiency. In addition to using internal assessments to identify the low performers who should be dismissed during a downsizing, employees can also be assessed in the competencies and capabilities the firm anticipates needing in the future. Employees who have the competencies the company needs to execute its business strategy or to create or maintain its competitive advantage may be retained, and employees lacking the characteristics and abilities the firm needs to succeed in the future may be the ones let go. In addition to assessing employee skills to make informed decisions about organizational structure and staffing during a downsizing effort, some companies also assess employees' desires to use those skills.[41]

Informing Restructuring Decisions

Restructuring involves reorganizing work to enhance the firm's strategic execution. This usually requires moving some employees to other positions, changing job requirements, and transitioning some employees out of the company. Both restructuring and downsizing decisions should be based on the business plan and take into consideration the ability of individual employees to contribute to the company. Understanding a company's profit-generating services and products, and how jobs and employees each contribute to them, makes employee reassignments more strategic and effective.

Internal Assessment Methods

The assessment methods described in the *Staffing Strategically Series* book titled *Assessing External Job Candidates*, including biographical information, structured interviews, simulations, assessment centers, and clinical assessments, can be just as useful for assessing internal job candidates. When an international medical-products supply company redefined its field sales managers' roles to better address the company's business challenges, it identified new competencies, behaviors, and performance standards. It then immersed current and potential field sales managers in simulations that reflected the changing nature and demands of their new roles to assess the fit between individual capabilities and future job requirements. It also provided a realistic preview of the position's new requirements and identified employees' strengths and development needs to ensure their capabilities matched their future role requirements.[42]

In addition to the assessment methods used with external applicants, there are a variety of assessment methods that can be used with internal job candidates. Because internal job candidates already work for the company, more, and richer, information is usually available. Although employees can be assessed by an outside contractor, informal methods that are conducted by the employee and supervisors can be equally effective and less costly.[43] We next discuss several commonly used initial, substantive, and discretionary internal assessment methods.

Initial Assessment Methods

There are several ways in which firms perform an initial assessment of internal job candidates, including skills inventories, mentoring programs, and succession management programs.

Skill Inventories. According to John Walker, global leader for HR at Dow Chemical Company, "A lot of organizations talk about their core competencies, but unless they measure them it can be difficult to know what they really are."[44] Skill inventories (or skill databases) allow a company to maintain a list of which employees have certain skills, competencies, and other relevant characteristics. When the firm needs a sales associate who speaks French, the database is simply queried. The skills required for each job can also be matched against current jobholders' skills, providing a training and development plan for each employee.

Some companies use sophisticated software systems to manage the process while others rely on paper or spreadsheets. Technology can assist in the effective compilation and presentation of this information, including modules from SAP, PeopleSoft, Oracle, and Saba Software. There are other, smaller specialty applications that can be purchased without the large investment usually required with these software applications. When kept in a database, this information can be quickly searched to assign employees to new projects or to help identify employees to consider for other positions. Some organizations hold employees responsible for keeping their skills inventories updated and accurate via the company's intranet. Once an employee possesses all of the qualifications required to be considered for another position, the software identifies them as ready to be considered when a vacancy arises.

The organization and its budget determine the number and types of skills tracked, and at what level of detail each is evaluated. Skills inventories can be limited to basic information obtained when the employee began working for the company, such as education, work experience, and any training or certifications completed, or they can be continually updated as employees acquire additional skills and qualifications. To be most useful for staffing purposes, it is important that skills inventories be accurate and current. Because the company determines what information is in a skills inventory, it can be a good strategic decision to identify and track, in appropriate detail, the competencies required for success in other positions, as well as characteristics related to person-organization fit. The better the information in a skills inventory relates to the prediction of performance in other jobs in the company, the more useful it is in assessing and screening employees. Before collecting any information for a talent inventory, it is important to clearly communicate to employees what information will be collected, how it will be used, and the privacy safeguards that are in place.

IBM considers skills to be a company asset, and keeps its skills inventory open to managers and employees. Managers can view and update files, and employees can view and update their own files. When forming teams, staff queries the inventory for complementary skills to find names, or scan for names to get skills.[45]

Mentoring Programs. Mentoring is "a dynamic, reciprocal relationship in a work environment between an advanced career incumbent (mentor) and a beginner (protégé) aimed at promoting the career development of both."[46] Mentoring relationships can be established through formal mentoring programs in which a mentor is assigned to an employee, or they can be informal and develop on their own.

Mentoring programs can be a good source of initial assessments and nominations of candidates, as well as a useful method of providing career enhancement for mentors and career progression for protégés. Mentors can be asked to nominate their protégés for positions they feel they are ready for. Coaching and social support can both positively influence managers' salary level and promotions.[47] Mentoring can also be an effective training tool for smaller companies that can't afford formal training programs.

Wachovia Executive Coaching Practice developed more than 70 internal coaches who mentor and support 189 leaders across the bank. These coaches perform 360-degree evaluations of participants' leadership competencies, create individual development plans, and provide ongoing support. In 2006, Wachovia estimated a business impact of more than $360,000 per coaching engagement.[48]

Managing Succession. Succession management is an ongoing process of systematically identifying, assessing, and developing organizational leadership to enhance performance.[49] Succession management involves ongoing strategic talent planning, retirement and retention planning, and talent assessment and development.[50] Succession management plans are written policies that guide the succession management process. Succession management can ensure leadership continuity, prevent key positions from remaining vacant after the incumbent leaves, prevent transition problems, and reduce incidents of premature promotion.

Succession management helps to deploy talent to enable the firm to meet its business goals. In response to changing organizational and employee needs, succession management can identify the current or potential availability of internal organization replacements for key positions.[51] Succession management plans should be put in place before they are needed, and can be very good investments.

When McDonald's CEO Jim Cantalupo died unexpectedly in 2004, he was replaced six hours later. A few weeks later, the replacement CEO, Charlie Bell, was diagnosed with cancer, and the board again made an orderly replacement.[52] On the other hand, when Frank Lanza, the chairman and CEO of defense contractor L-3 Communications, passed away at age 74, the company hadn't prepared for it. The board took three days just to name an interim chief executive, and the company was widely speculated to be a takeover target because of the leadership crisis.[53]

Although succession management can expedite the process of replacing a departing employee, employees identified by succession management as candidates for an open position should not be the only employees considered for the job. Information about an opening should generally be disseminated to all employees to give them the opportunity to apply in case some talent is being overlooked. It is important to ensure that information about position openings does not become a secretive, employee-alienating situation. It is obviously not ideal for an employee who would have been interested in a job opportunity in the company to not learn of the vacancy and miss the opportunity. When done well, succession planning not only helps future managers and top executives prepare for their positions, but reinforces a company culture and talent philosophy that believes in treating employees as investors rather than assets.

Succession management requires much more than simply identifying which employees might be able to assume a particular position should an opening occur. Effective succession management builds a series of feeder groups across the entire leadership pipeline.[54] In contrast, replacement planning is narrowly focused on identifying specific back-up candidates for specific senior management positions and does little to improve leadership readiness. Succession management is a key driver of employee retention and sends a signal to the firm's stakeholders that the firm's leadership is preparing for the future.[55] Replacement planning is helpful for quickly identifying a possible successor when a position unexpectedly opens.

Succession management should integrate talent management with the organization's strategic plan. Companies must identify and meet staffing goals that support the organization's long-term direction, growth, and planned change. Replacements may need different competencies, values, and experiences than incumbents. Strategically managing succession should enable an organization to have the right people in the right place at the right time to execute the business strategy. With the impending retirement of Baby Boomers and increased demands for diversity, many organizations are building systems that provide talented high performers opportunities to grow. PanCanadian Petroleum actively tries to identify "bright lights" and employees who possess critical skills, and scans the entire organization for high-potential young managers.[56]

Organizations often integrate workforce diversity into succession management.[57] Allstate has successfully used succession management to ensure that it identifies and develops diverse slates of qualified candidates for all key positions. Allstate assesses all employees' current job skills and creates roadmaps for developing the required competencies for advancement within the company. Development options made available to employees include education, coaching and mentoring, classroom training, and a variety of career experiences.[58]

To open up the promotion process and relieve the concerns of women and minorities, who often feel shut out of promotion opportunities, Kodak's Leadership Assessment and Development Center began an open-door program to develop anyone interesting in being considered for a supervisory position. This approach enhances the perceived fairness of the promotion process, and the experience helps many employees realize that they are not interested in higher-level jobs after all. After attending the introductory course "So You Want to Be a Leader?" about 25 percent of participants "deselect" themselves. After the second course, which gave instruction on handling supervisory duties, including budgeting, staffing, and production, another 25 percent tend to drop out.[59]

If done strategically, succession management can help ensure that at least one internal candidate is able to quickly assume a key position should it become vacant. This can save the organization considerable lost productivity and expense for the time it would otherwise take to identify and possibly train a replacement from inside or outside the company, and it can also help retain talented employees who might otherwise leave to pursue higher-level positions at other organizations. Because succession management plans need to be revised as jobs and employees change, it can be a time-consuming process and is typically done only for key positions in the organization.

Health benefits company WellPoint is a good example of a successful succession management program. The company wanted to do a better job identifying and tracking the development of promising internal talent, and enabling top management to evaluate candidates across the company's locations. To do this, WellPoint combined succession management and performance appraisals in an annual process that allows it to quickly identify a list of candidates and assess who might be the best fit for job openings. Each of the 600 participants in its succession plan annually writes a self-evaluation to which his or her supervisor adds a performance appraisal, core competency rating, and an assessment of the employee's potential for promotion. The supervisor also indicates who might be capable of replacing the employee if he or she is promoted. That data is combined with other employee characteristics such as education, language skills, and experience to create employee profiles that are then assembled into succession charts.[60] WellPoint's succession-planning software also allows for detailed queries that let it evaluate employees' fit with different job opportunities that arise.[61]

WellPoint also prepares its future succession candidates with an integrated training and career development program. Because WellPoint fills more than 85 percent of its management positions internally, it saves hundreds of thousands of dollars annually on executive search expenses and fills executive positions in an average of 35 days. WellPoint estimates that using the succession management system has saved more than $21 million in recruitment and training expenses and reduced managerial turnover by six percent.[62]

WellPoint is also able to spot problematic areas in its succession chart, allowing it to develop initiatives to build bench strength in those areas before they cause problems. It also uses its database to identify lateral opportunities as a tool for assessing core competencies within the organization, and to identify where it needs to focus its development and training resources.[63]

Although WellPoint does not provide details about the overall cost of its succession-planning program or the return on its investment, it estimates that it saved $1 million when it filled two top-level executive positions internally and then "backfilled" each resulting vacancy with internal candidates going down five management levels.[64]

Steps in Developing a Succession Management Plan. After choosing the position on which to focus, the first general step in a succession management project is the assessment of current and future competencies, behaviors, and values needed for high performance in the key position. Jobs change over time, and the competencies that will be needed in the future incumbent must be identified to ensure that candidates are properly selected and developed. For example, if the organization is planning to change its culture to become more service-oriented, customer service competencies need to be added to the job requirements matrix and job specification. If technology will become more integrated with the position, technology skills should be added. As people move up in an organization, new ways of managing and leading are needed in terms of: (1) the capabilities required to execute the new responsibilities; (2) new time frames governing how one works; and (3) work values or what is believed to be important and is the focus of one's effort.[65]

The second general step in a succession management project is to identify—through formal assessment centers and skills testing, or more informally via supervisory assessments—each identified and interested candidate's strengths, weaknesses, and succession readiness. When a key position becomes vacant, creating and maintaining a database of employee competencies and succession readiness can facilitate and expedite the succession process by matching eligible employees with the open position.

Maintenance of skill inventory records can be burdensome, but it is a critical task in succession management to avoid overlooking qualified internal candidates. One of the barriers to successfully maintaining these records is the volume of information that is sometimes requested of the managers responsible for updating the system. If the system is user-friendly and only data relevant to making advancement decisions is collected, then this burden is reduced.

The final general step in succession management is to create a plan to continually and systematically improve the capabilities of all identified succession candidates. This requires that succession management be thought of as a continuous process, not something that is done only once or twice a year. Using the assessment of candidates' competencies, training programs and development opportunities can be identified to increase candidates' readiness for the key positions. If candidates are informed of areas in which further development would help prepare them for their targeted positions, they can be active partners in systematically building the competencies needed to be effective in their next position with the company.

Corporate intranets can be used to keep employee skill profiles and job interests available for easy reference when positions become available or when succession planning is being done. Enabling employees to access their profiles can help ensure that the information is updated and accurate, and can make employees active partners in the succession management process. A thorough and updated database of skill profiles greatly facilitates the identification and recruitment of qualified candidates for future job openings. Table 3 summarizes the steps involved in developing an effective succession management system.

In addition to expediting the replacement of talent in key positions, succession management has other benefits. The outcomes of the succession management process include the engagement of management in a disciplined review of existing leadership talent in the organization, and a leadership inventory of current talent. Another outcome is the identification of potential gaps in the capabilities, skills, and leadership of current employees relative to the future talent needs of the organization. If the succession management process fails to identify qualified internal candidates for the target position, action plans need to be developed to remedy the talent gap. Understanding the nature of talent gaps—before the talent is actually needed—can allow the organization to:

- Plan for and remedy any workforce talent deficiencies;
- Develop an external recruiting strategy to bring in external talent;
- Redesign the work to reduce the need for the talent expected to be in short supply; and
- Give the organization time to develop internal talent by providing additional training programs and creating opportunities for employees to practice those skills.

Table 3. Steps in Developing a Succession Management System

1. Assess current and future competencies, behaviors, values, etc., needed for future job performance in the chosen position.
2. Assess each identified and interested candidate's strengths, weaknesses, and readiness to move into other positions.
3. Create a plan to continually and systematically improve the capabilities of all identified succession candidates.
4. Create a plan to identify qualified and interested internal candidates for open positions.
5. Evaluate the system on relevant criteria, including the number of positions filled with candidates who have been the target of succession management activities.
6. Continually improve the system.

Succession management may reveal a larger number of interested and qualified internal candidates for a target position than was expected or realistically needed by the organization. This knowledge can help an organization plan alternate career paths for the surplus talent, helping to prevent the turnover of these employees when they do not get the promotions for which they are ready. Understanding the nature of an organization's talent pool can also inform the organization's strategic planning process by identifying whether it has the depth of talent required to execute various strategic alternatives. For example, if a regional clothing store is planning to expand nationally, knowing that it has substantial potential store-manager talent in its existing associate store-manager employee ranks can be a prerequisite for opening the new stores. If the succession planning of store managers indicates that internal store-manager talent is in short supply, the organization can make hiring employees with the potential to become store managers a key goal of its recruiting and hiring process, or plan to hire store managers for the new locations from outside of the company. If done far enough in advance, succession management can facilitate an organization's business strategy execution and even influence the choice of which business strategy to pursue (if, of course, it does not have the talent available to execute some of its strategic options).

Effective Succession Management Systems. Fairness and open communication are critical components of succession management. The process should be impartial, open, and backed by top management. Employees should be able to express an interest in being considered for positions that appeal to them, and should not be coerced into pursuing positions in which they are not interested. Not everyone wants to be in a leadership position, and employees pressured into jobs they do not truly want are more likely to leave the organization. Feedback from as many sources as is reasonable (e.g., objective, multirater assessments) should be used in evaluating an employee's skills and candidacy for another position. Incorporating feedback and creating "buy-in" among key constituencies are also important cornerstones of successful succession management systems.

Skills inventories and nominating employees for consideration for the targeted positions rely on the cooperation and participation of supervisors who are not always highly motivated to lose their best employees to other positions in the organization. Some managers perceive greater personal rewards for keeping their best people and not nominating them for opportunities elsewhere in the organization. If a manager continually invests time in developing his or her best subordinates for positions elsewhere in the organization, and encourages them to pursue the positions they are interested in, this creates more work for the manager and compromises the performance of his or her own workgroup by continually cycling out the best performing members. Some managers may even believe that they are grooming their own successors and hastening their own departure from the organization.

Other managers derive intrinsic rewards from developing and mentoring employees to move up in an organization.

Managers' involvement and commitment is critical to the success of the succession management process because their skills assessments, promotability ratings, and development activities are central to the preparation of identified candidates for the new positions. Incentives for managers to do a good job identifying and developing high-potential talent can help secure their commitment, and it is important that managers perceive greater rewards in identifying and developing their best talent for other positions in the organization than in keeping them on their own teams. When Warner-Lambert's HR senior-leadership team prepared a set of principles as part of a redesign of its practices, the first principle stated, "Talent across the company is managed for the larger interests of the company. Our divisions are the stewards of that talent, and company-wide interests prevail."[66] Communicating and reinforcing strong, clear statements of this nature to managers throughout the company improves understanding and buy-in to the idea of talent being the company's (rather than a manager's) asset. Including succession management in all managers' performance appraisals and tying their development of future leadership talent to financial rewards and promotions also helps align managers' goals with those of the organization.

The succession management process needs to make sense to, and be usable by, different business units. A standardized process can help to focus and guide the development of employees to meet the strategic needs of the organization, and increase employee perceptions of the program's fairness by reducing opportunities for favoritism. The process should also align with other HR processes, including recruitment, selection, rewards, training, and performance management. For example, if the current succession plan for a position indicates that the organization lacks depth in a particular talent, adjustments to the recruitment and selection system can bring more of that talent into the organization. Performance management systems can be modified to assess employees on the competencies they need to be qualified for other positions as well as on their performance in their current jobs. Succession management can help an organization deal with diversity issues and changing demographics by making promotion opportunities more available to a greater number of people in the organization. The best succession plans bridge the gap between individual career development opportunities and long-term business strategy. Because organizations constantly change, succession plans and the succession management process should be continuously reviewed and modified. The process should be designed to be ongoing, fluid, and adaptable to shifting and emerging contexts.

Work assignments and other development activities need to be regularly assigned to succession candidates, and employees' skills inventories and readiness for consideration for targeted transfer opportunities need to be continually updated. The best succession management programs include development activities and focus on identifying and enhancing the competencies the candidate will need to be successful in the transfer position. By increasing the pool of talent that will be qualified for key positions in the future, succession management ultimately facilitates the execution of the organization's business strategy.

Some firms prefer to call employees targeted for accelerated development through succession management and career development programs "acceleration pools" rather than "high-potential pools" because the latter term implies that employees not in the pool are not high potential.[67] Because the definition of "high potential" can change as business requirements and goals change, and to avoid alienating employees who are not labeled "high potential," Yahoo! avoids calling any employees high potential. The firm's executive training program is offered not only to individuals identified as promotion candidates, but to other employees as well. Nonetheless, Yahoo! pays special attention to its stars and focuses on the training and career development of select employees to reduce the chances that these key employees will leave. Leadership potential is also identified through performance reviews and at an annual session held by senior executives.[68]

Continually evaluating the success of a succession management program is important in ensuring its effectiveness at meeting the organization's succession goals. One large organization boasted having a succession management process, but after analyzing the data about the program's success, it realized that virtually no senior managers ever came out of it. Clearly, some other subjective criteria were being used to determine promotions, which risks demoralizing good employees and increasing their turnover.[69]

Company executives need to both model effective succession-management behaviors and hold line managers responsible for developing their subordinates' skills and knowledge (e.g., by including talent development in annual evaluations). However, data suggests that many companies fail to do this. One survey found that nearly half of respondents felt their organization's senior leadership does not align talent-management strategies with business strategies, and that senior managers do not spend enough time on talent management. Fifty-two percent of the respondents identified line managers' insufficient commitment to developing talent as a critical barrier to effective succession management. Furthermore, 50 percent observed that line managers were unwilling to categorize their people as top, average, or underperforming, and 45 percent felt that line managers failed to deal with chronic underperformance by employees.[70] Many well-designed succession management systems fail to live up to their potential because of a lack of commitment on the part of executives and line managers.

Table 4 provides some tips for effective succession management.

Substantive Assessment Methods

After making initial screening decisions of which internal candidates to consider further for the position, substantive assessment methods are used to perform more in-depth evaluations. We next discuss a variety of commonly used substantive internal assessment methods.

Performance Reviews. In addition to actual performance outcomes, which can be influenced by factors beyond employees' control, the task and interpersonal behaviors employees engage in are also important to assess, as these reflect both competencies and work styles. Performance reviews (also called performance appraisals) can be limited to feedback from a supervisor to an employee, or involve multiple sources of ratings, including customers, peers, and subordinates.[71] Ratings from nonsupervisors are generally used only for employee development and performance evaluations, and promotion and transfer decisions are usually informed by supervisor ratings.

Table 4. Succession Management Tips

Here are some experts' recommendations for creating and maintaining an effective succession management system:

- *Keep the process simple.* Make the process logical and simple so that busy line managers do not feel that the process is burdensome.[i]
- *Use technology to support the process.* Information technology enables the timely monitoring and updating of developmental needs and activities.[ii]
- *Align succession management with overall business strategy.* Top executives and line managers will be more supportive of a system that clearly reinforces corporate goals and objectives.[iii]
- *Focus on development.* Succession management must be a flexible system oriented toward developmental activities rather than a list of high-potential employees and future positions they might fill.[iv]
- *Model effective succession management behaviors at the top.* Company executives need to both model effective succession management behaviors and hold line managers responsible for developing their subordinates' skills and knowledge.[v]
- *Approach succession management as a key business activity.* Because of its key role in enabling long-term business strategy execution, succession management should be incorporated into hiring and developing employees, as well as assigning them to projects, training, and other development activities.[vi]

[i] Fulmer, R.M., "Choose Tomorrow's Leaders Today," *Graziadio Business Report*, Winter 2002, available online at: gbr.pepperdine.edu/021/succession.html. Accessed January 16, 2009. [ii] Ibid. [iii] Ibid. [iv] Conger, J.A. & Fulmer, R.M., "Developing Your Leadership Pipeline," *Harvard Business Review*, December 2003, pp. 76-84. [v] Guthridge, M., Komm, A.B., & Lawson, E., "The People Problem in Talent Management," *The McKinsey Quarterly*, October 26, 2006, available online at: www.mckinseyquarterly.com/article_page.aspx?ar=1755&L2=18&L3=31&srid=63&gp=1. Accessed January 16, 2009. [vi] Metzler, J.C., "Planning For Transition," American Institute of Certified Public Accountants, August 2005, Vol. 7, available online at: pcps.aicpa.org/NR/rdonlyres/42B0698A-4576-4795-AEDC-DD7E3DF5E94B/0/SFCvolume7final.pdf. Accessed January 12, 2009.

As shown in Figure 2, multisource assessments (sometimes called 360-degree assessments) involve the employee's supervisor, as well as other sources who are familiar with an employee's job performance. These sources typically include the employee, subordinates, peers, and even internal and external customers. These sources can be used alone or together in assessing an employee, and should be weighted based on their credibility and ability to observe and accurately rate the employee's behaviors. We next discuss each of the sources in more detail.

Figure 2. Multisource Assessments

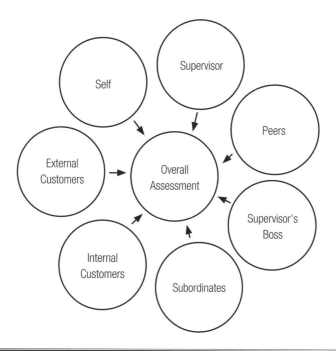

Employees generally expect feedback from their supervisor and prefer using him or her as the main source of performance appraisals.[72] Supervisors can assess such factors as an employee's current job performance, strengths, development needs, promotion potential, and specific competencies. To spot good promotion candidates who may have been overlooked or underestimated by their supervisor, WellPoint sets up "challenge sessions" in which supervisors in a group scrutinize one another's evaluations.[73]

An employee's supervisor is often the person most familiar with and responsible for an employee's job-performance outcomes, but may be less able to see the employee's task and interpersonal behaviors. Although supervisors are commonly the primary (if not only) source of performance information, it is not clear that this is the optimal practice—people other than the supervisor may be better qualified to evaluate the employee's interpersonal and task behaviors.[74] Also, if a supervisor has never hired people for his or her own level, his or her assessments of an employee's promotability likely need to be confirmed by the supervisor's boss. The supervisor's boss also oversees that the supervisor has been diligent in conducting the performance assessment. Using performance reviews that incorporate evaluations of promotability and professional development plans can improve the usefulness of supervisor assessments. We next discuss several other sources of performance-appraisal information.

Asking employees to assess their own performance and capabilities can also be useful. In addition to improving communication between employees and their supervisors, self-assessments help to identify areas where an employee feels that they could benefit from additional coaching or development. When a supervisor cannot easily observe work behaviors and outcomes, self-assessments can be particularly valuable. Although employees are obviously in the best position to observe their interpersonal and task behaviors, a limitation of self-assessments is the fact that people aren't always good judges of their own talents. Some high performers tend to rate themselves lower than do other raters, and others rate themselves too high.[75] The key reasons to include self-evaluations are to allow the employee to provide performance documentation that the supervisor or others don't have, and to allow the employee to convey professional development goals and desired career tracks to the firm.

When work is done in teams or when employees act interdependently in getting their work done, peers are often the most knowledgeable about their co-workers' performance. The amount and type of work contact an evaluator has with the person being assessed is important because raters can only accurately rate those aspects of a person's work performance that they observe.[76] Supervisors, peers, and subordinates see different aspects of a person's work behaviors and performance.[77] Although peers tend to get a good look at each others' task and interpersonal behaviors, peers tend to be more willing to rate each other honestly when the ratings are used for developmental purposes rather than evaluative purposes (e.g., for feedback and development purposes rather than to determine pay, promotion, or retention outcomes). Peer ratings have also been found to be valid when predicting promotion criteria,[78] although peer ratings are often less reliable than supervisor ratings.[79] To reduce the influence of politics and friendships, it is important that peers understand the characteristics required for success and be familiar with the job requirements matrix for the position. As is done with Olympic judges, some companies eliminate the lowest and highest peer ratings and average the rest.[80] Employees can be asked to assess each peer's promotion readiness or to rank order or vote for which peers are the most promotable. Some firms ask employees to nominate peers they feel would be good candidates for openings. For peer ratings to be effective, employees must accept the peer-rating process and believe that it is fair.[81]

Asking subordinates to appraise their managers is often the most controversial feature of a multisource assessment program. Although subordinates may not see all of their boss' task behaviors, they very often see their supervisors' interpersonal and leadership behaviors and thus have a unique and important perspective on his or her managerial behaviors, strengths, and limitations. One limitation of subordinate feedback is that subordinates are often reluctant or even afraid to give their supervisors negative feedback. Rater anonymity is critical, but if subordinates feel that their responses might be identifiable (i.e., if the supervisor has only a few subordinates), or if they fear reprisal, then subordinate ratings are not likely to be accurate.

Internal customers are users of any products or services supplied by another employee or group within the same organization. External customers are those outside the firm, including other companies and the general public. Both internal and external customers have a moderate opportunity to observe employees' task and interpersonal behaviors, and their feedback helps to incorporate the perspective of the company's stakeholders beyond the typical chain of command. Because employees are rewarded for satisfying the expectations of the people who control their compensation, incorporating customer feedback expands the range of stakeholders employees seek to please.

Because external customers do not see or understand the work processes and rules that influence employees' task behaviors, they often cannot easily separate an employee's task behaviors from the regulations, policies, and resources that direct and constrain the employee's options.[82] As a result, it can be best to ask external customers to evaluate interpersonal behaviors. Nonetheless, internal and external customer assessments can help identify a company's strategic capabilities and assess how well employees are executing the business strategy. Table 5 summarizes the frequency with which each rating source is able to observe task and interpersonal behaviors.

Table 5. Observation Frequency of Task and Interpersonal Behaviors for Different Raters

	Self	Supervisor	Subordinates	Peers	Internal Customers	External Customers
Task Behaviors	High	Medium	Low	Medium to High	Medium	Low
Interpersonal Behaviors	High	Low	Medium to High	Medium to High	Medium	Medium

Consulting firm Booz Allen Hamilton's Employee Development Frameworks identify required competencies and appropriate development opportunities at each step of the career ladder. Employees receive competency maps, individual development plans, and a 360-degree annual competency assessment involving consultations with as many as 15 colleagues. The firm ties promotions to competency development and business needs.[83]

Job Knowledge Tests. Job knowledge tests can be as useful for internal assessment as they are for external assessment. Because well-developed and validated job knowledge tests can measure a person's knowledge, experience, cognitive ability, and motivation to learn, they can help to predict which employees will perform the best in an open position. Many organizations, including police departments, use job knowledge tests to assess candidates being considered for promotion. At the U.S. Department of Homeland Security, evaluating employees for promotion to some special agent positions involves a five-hour test battery that includes a job knowledge test assessing technical skills; a critical thinking test; and an in-basket exercise that measures leadership competencies, including planning, prioritizing, work scheduling, and delegating work. Applicants passing this test battery take a writing skills assessment and participate in a structured interview.[84]

Discretionary Assessment Methods

Discretionary internal assessment methods are those typically reserved for the much smaller pool of finalists left over after performing initial and substantive assessments. The two discretionary assessment methods used most often for internal candidates are assessment centers and clinical assessment.

Assessment Centers. Assessment centers measure job candidates' knowledge, skills, abilities, and competencies by putting them through a series of simulations and exercises that reflect job content and typical job challenges. Assessment centers also often include cognitive ability tests, personality assessments, and job knowledge tests. The tendency for assessment centers to result in adverse impact, or disproportionate hiring rates for different ethnic or gender subgroups, varies depending on the exercises used.

Because Cessna Aircraft Company has fewer people doing more work than it used to, it feels that it can't afford to make a bad hiring decision. The company wants to have a good look at how people will do the job before it hires them. Cessna's Independence plant uses an elaborate role-playing exercise for managers, which simulates a "day in the life" of a busy executive. A job candidate spends as many as 12 hours in an office with a phone, fax, and in-basket stuffed with files and letters. Throughout the day, the job candidate works through memos and handles problems such as a phone call from an angry customer.[85]

Because of their high cost relative to other assessment methods, assessment centers are used more for managerial and higher-level jobs. Many of the skills and competencies assessment centers evaluate can also be assessed by giving employees the opportunity to demonstrate managerial talent by being a project team leader or committee chair. Assessment centers can also assess external candidates. Assessment centers seem to work in a variety of organizational settings, and can be useful for selection and promotion decisions as well as training, career planning, and for improving managerial skills.

Clinical Assessment. Clinical assessments rely on trained psychologists to subjectively analyze a candidate's attributes, values, and styles in the context of a particular job. Clinical assessments are based on ability and personality tests, interviews, information about the candidate's personal history, and direct observations of behavior. The clinical assessment is usually presented as a written description of the candidate, and may or may not contain a clear hire/don't hire recommendation.[86] Because clinical assessments are expensive, and not consistent in what they assess or how they are done, their validity is unknown. They tend to be used for higher-level positions such as executives and CEOs who have greater power and influence in the company and for whom job descriptions may be more flexible. In these cases, companies sometimes use a psychologist to try to evaluate a candidate's strengths and weaknesses and determine the broad impact a candidate would likely have on the organization.

Career Planning

Career planning is a continuous process of career-oriented self-assessment and goal setting.[87] When integrated with the organization's succession management and labor-forecasting processes, career planning and succession management can help give any organization a snapshot of available talent for meeting current and future needs.[88]

In the career planning process, the goals, preferences, and capabilities of employees are assessed via interest inventories, interviews, assessment centers, etc. The current and future needs of the organization based on the HR strategy and succession plan are then compared to the talents and motivations of employees, and the degree of match or mismatch is discussed with each individual. For employees identified as candidates for other positions, career development opportunities are identified that build the competencies and talents required to achieve the individual's future goals. Kimberly-Clark provides broad and diverse career paths for its employees, allowing employees to develop their careers through increased responsibility, expertise, or leadership, or through cross-functional opportunities.[89]

Organizations can increase employee retention and the depth of talent available for leadership positions by integrating the career planning and succession management processes, and by linking them to organizational goals and strategies. By helping individuals match their career interests with realistic career opportunities in the organization in which they currently work, career planning can reduce employees' perceptions that they need to leave the organization to accomplish their career goals.

To be strategic, career planning needs to complement the expected future talent needs of the organization. For example, if an organization expects to expand in the next 10 years, career planning can help identify current employees who are willing to pursue advancement opportunities in the company and help it execute its expansion goals. If employees feel that the organization is proactively trying to understand their needs and interests and match them to other positions, their commitment to the organization may increase. On the other hand, if employees perceive promotions to be determined in subjective or political ways, they may be more likely to leave the organization, particularly if they are passed over for promotion. Career planning can increase the motivation of the organization's best talent to stay in the organization because they perceive a rewarding future with the company. If high-potential employees feel that the only way to advance their careers is to leave the organization, the organization is likely to have a shortage of promotion-ready employees from which to draw in the future. If a company's top talent feels that the organization is pressuring them to pursue positions in which they are not interested, they may also leave the company. If in the future the organization wishes to promote from within the organization rather than hire from outside the company for its managerial ranks, the needed talent may not be available.

Too often succession management is done without telling the identified employees that the organization recognizes their potential. An organization's high-potential talent pool should be informed of their status in the company and should know that the organization has its eye on them for advancement in the company. Career planning helps to facilitate this and coordinate employees' personal goals with the organization's needs. General Mills tailors each employee's career development to his or her professional needs, long-term aspirations, and potential for personal growth. Formal training plans to enhance employees' performance in their current roles are combined with individual development plans that also build capabilities for future roles.[90] Communications provider Cox Communications begins its talent review process by gathering information on the employee's career interest and willingness to relocate. Managers provide feedback to their employees through a series of review meetings, and then work with them to create a development plan based on the identified needs.[91]

As with succession management, the career planning process should be evaluated and improved as the needs of the organization and employees change. Because employees need to stay with the organization long enough to transition into the other positions for the succession management and career planning processes to be worthwhile, the return on the career planning and succession management investment is obviously greater for organizations with lower levels of employee turnover. By showing employees that their career goals can be reached within the organization, turnover could also be reduced after the implementation of integrated career planning and succession management programs.

Many career development tools are available to expand and improve employees' skill sets and prepare them to be competitive for other positions in the organization. These tools increase the probability that future internal recruitment efforts will be successful, and include:

Assessment centers, which simulate the position an employee is interested in pursuing, help both the organization and the employee evaluate whether the individual is a good potential fit with the position. Although expensive, assessment centers can be very effective at identifying an individual's strengths and areas for improvement, and do a fairly good job predicting candidates' likely success in a particular position.[92]

- Career counseling and career development workshops help individuals understand the jobs that best match their motivations and talents, and help them develop the skills they need to successfully compete for these opportunities.
- Training and continuing education can provide skills training in a more formalized educational setting.
- Job rotation, challenging assignments, and mentoring can provide skill development in a more informal manner.
- Sabbaticals can be used to give employees the opportunity to develop skills and pursue other potential interests that allow them to return to the job re-energized. Professional associations are also a source of continuing education and conferences, and workshops can be used to build skills and investigate other career opportunities.
- Challenging and developmental job assignments can enhance key competencies and build experience in important job tasks before the individual assumes the position.

Challenging job assignments are one of the best career development tools.[93] However, it is common for organizations to seek to fill challenging assignments with people able to do the job well right now rather than to consider the assignment an opportunity for career development. Common barriers to using challenging job assignments for career development include the belief that moving people around and taking them away from their current job responsibilities is not worth the disruption, and a lack of clarity about what skills should be developed in whom and what learning opportunities the job assignment offers.[94] Because people learn when they are put in situations that require skills they do not currently have, organizations should consider using challenging job assignments as part of their career-development process. Some organizations have a formal system to evaluate the development potential of project and job assignments and strategically assign them to fast-tracked talent.

The Hartford Financial Services Group has a Corporate University web site that employees and their managers can search by subject, competency, course title, etc., to identify development opportunities. Employees can also use the company intranet to look up job families, identify possible advancement paths, and identify the differences in expectations, responsibilities, and competencies required by different career paths. This allows employees and their managers to better identify what competencies need to be developed to progress.[95]

Succession Management and Career Planning Implementation. Assist and encourage employees to decide for themselves where they want their careers to go. Employees' articulated interests and intentions should always be respected—someone should never be forced into an unwanted promotion, even if that person is the best internal candidate. American Greetings interviews all high-potential employees to determine what they like and dislike about their jobs and what their individual goals are. Because people's goals and ambitions can change over time, the developmental plan is put in place even if an employee claims to have no interest in advancement. American Greetings' primary objective is to make its high-potential employees more effective in the jobs they already have.[96]

An organization's succession management and career planning processes should be thoroughly integrated with its other human resource functions and systems. Convincing supervisors to take time from their busy schedules to provide evaluative information about their subordinates' skills and readiness for other positions can be particularly challenging. Keeping a skills database updated and accurate requires the commitment and buy-in of busy people, and the nomination of their best talent for other positions is not necessarily consistent with managers' own goals for the high performance of their own workgroup. Emphasizing follow through and accountability for these managers is important if a career planning and succession management initiative is to succeed.

It is important to examine the alignment of existing HR management systems such as recruitment, selection, training, compensation, and benefits against succession management and development efforts, and to identify any HR management practices that presently encourage or discourage effective succession management and development. If rewards only exist for workgroup performance and not for identifying and developing talent for other positions in the organization, the organization is essentially communicating to managers that it is not committed to succession management and employee development. If an organization's external recruitment and selection systems do not result in talented and promotable new hires, the succession management and career development programs will have very little raw material with which to work and the talent pipeline is likely to stay weak regardless of the organization's commitment to promotion from within.

Forecasts for business and headcount growth or decline should be taken into account when succession and career planning. If an organization is restructuring, it is possible that some of the positions for which succession had been planned will be eliminated. Ensuring that managers give specific consideration to the long-term retention and development of high-potential employees even during periods of reorganization or downsizing is important to keep a strong leadership and talent pipeline. Identifying any disincentives that exist that dissuade employees from wanting to accept promotions or assume leadership roles can also improve the effectiveness of the career planning and succession management initiative. For example, if employees tend to perceive a particular promotion as unattractive because it requires longer hours, greater responsibility, and very little additional pay, addressing these issues can increase the desirability of the position. It is important to remember that career planning and succession management are processes, not events, and require continual attention to be effective and contribute to the organization's ability to execute its business strategy.

As an example of a company that has successfully integrated its succession management and career planning processes, Delta Air Lines' Human Resource Planning process integrates employees' career interests, skills, and abilities—as well as their perceptions of their own job performance with their managers' assessments of their performance and experiences—to assess promotability, possible next moves, strengths, and development needs. During review meetings, these managerial assessments are calibrated and validated, and succession plans for all executive positions are reviewed. Managers then provide feedback to their employees and work with them to create an appropriate development plan. The highest-potential employees receive a year of focused development and special exposure opportunities. The success of Delta's Human Resource Planning process is evaluated by tracking promotions according to succession plans, the diversity mix of those identified as promotable, and the retention of high-potential employees.[97] Colgate-Palmolive uses its performance-management process and each employee's individual development plan to identify high-potential talent at the local, regional, and global levels. When considering staffing a position, Colgate-Palmolive doesn't consider only what the business needs, but also the development needs of various candidates to round out each candidate's overall experience.[98]

Measuring and developing talent is always at the forefront of General Electric's business strategy discussions. GE's operating system, referred to as its "learning culture in action," entails year-round learning sessions where leaders from GE and outside companies share knowledge and focus on generating the best ideas and practices. Conversations about developing talent and reaching business objectives run parallel to create a continuous link. Harry Elsinga, manager of Executive Development at GE, notes, "We really have a tight organization around how we combine our leadership meetings and how we approach our business. We have a constant cycle going on throughout the year where we talk about business and people at the same time. How do we develop talent in those businesses, how do we make sure that we have the right people to open a particular plant or to do an acquisition, etc.? Those discussions always go hand in hand. And it's not a one-time kind of conversation; this is a constant, ongoing process."[99]

Internal Assessment Models

Career Crossroads Model

When Walt Mahler was involved in the design of General Electric's succession management process in the early 1970s, he found that different leadership levels in an organization require different sets of competencies and values.[100] Mahler concluded that the most successful leaders change their perspective on what is important as they move to higher levels of leadership. For example, a finance manager has to see his or her role differently when managing the finance function than when managing the entire business unit. If a business-unit leader does not broaden his or her view of finance as the most critical aspect of his or her job, the leader will not master the additional nonfinance aspects of the business. It can be very difficult for individuals to change their perspective of what is important after years of schooling and work experience, but a leader's values and priorities must change to fit the enhanced breadth of each new position.

The focus of the career crossroads model is on manager and leadership positions rather than technical or professional work. The natural hierarchy of work that exists in most large, decentralized business organizations consists of six career passages from the entry level to the top job, with each passage representing increased complexity. The six passages are:

Starting Point: Managing yourself
- Passage 1: Managing others
- Passage 2: Managing managers
- Passage 3: Managing a function
- Passage 4: Managing a business
- Passage 5: Managing multiple businesses
- Passage 6: Managing the enterprise

Each passage requires learning new values and skills, and unlearning old ones. One of the biggest talent mistakes organizations can make is to promote people based solely on their mastery of their current position rather than on their potential and readiness to assume the responsibilities and adopt the values of the next leadership level. New leaders should be ready to assume most of the core responsibilities of the new position, although some continued development and coaching is generally required. Effective succession management should produce an abundance of high-performing, high-potential talent to draw from for each leadership level. Because the career crossroads model takes a long-term perspective, it enhances the organization's ability to create its own leadership talent from a broad talent base rather than relying on the identification and hiring of external star performers to fill leadership positions.

In smaller organizations, the number of leadership layers is reduced, but the skills required of leaders are similar. Managing others rather than solely managing oneself is the most common transition, and one that many people find difficult. In very small organizations, the owner typically manages everyone else in the company, but, in medium-sized companies, there may be a middle layer of management in which managers or supervisors are managed. Depending on the organization's needs and structure, functional managers may exist, and the owner acts as the CEO. Smaller organizations are also unlikely to have the luxury of a large number of employees to choose from when a leadership position opens. Nonetheless, succession management can be even more critical for business survival in smaller organizations as the departure of even one key person can cripple the organization if a successor is not found quickly.

Nine-Box Matrix

A nine-box matrix is a combined assessment of an employee's performance and potential. Many *Fortune* 500 companies, including Bank of America, GE, and Medco Health Solutions, use some variety of the nine-box matrix for classifying their managers' current job performance and potential for advancement. The matrix often reflects employees' evaluations on the basis of performance, corporate values, and perceived potential. An individual who is performing well may not be judged as highly as someone who has not delivered comparable results but has persevered in a real stretch assignment.[101]

Figure 3 illustrates the nine-box matrix and the different combinations of current job performance and likely future potential assessments.

Notice that an employee rated an exceptional performer but who is not likely to grow beyond his or her current position is rated lower (4) than an employee who is only fully performing but who is eligible for promotion (3).

The value of the nine-box matrix depends on the quality of the assessment methodology that determines the box each individual is placed in. The nine-box matrix is a method for displaying judgments made about employees, not for making those judgments. It can help companies understand the overall strength of their bench, but only if the employees were accurately evaluated in the first place.[102]

Figure 3. Nine-Box Matrix

		Current Job Performance		
		Exceptional	Fully Performing	Not Yet Fully Performing
Likely Future Potential	Eligible for Promotion	1 Exceptional performer ready to be promoted; should be promoted quickly as he or she is also at risk of leaving	3 Full performer capable of being promoted but with room to improve in current job; focus on improving current performance to enable a future promotion	6 Recently moved to this job and may eventually be good candidate for promotion
	Room for Growth in Current Position	2 Exceptional performer not yet ready for promotion; should be developed further to prepare for future promotion	5 Full performer with room to grow in current position; focus on performance improvement	8 Performs some parts of job poorly but should continue to grow in current position; identify reasons for underperformance and further develop skills
	Not Likely to Grow Beyond Current Position	4 Exceptional performer not likely to grow beyond scope of current position; consider involving them in the training of others	7 Full performer not likely to grow beyond scope of current position; coach and develop to improve both performance and potential	9 Underperformer not likely to grow beyond scope of current position; identify reasons for low performance and consider reassignment to a lower level or transitioning employee out of the company

Adapted from Charan, R., Drotter, S., & Noel, J., *The Leadership Pipeline: How to Build the Leadership-Powered Company*, 2001, San Francisco: Jossey-Bass.

Summary

The success of internal recruitment depends in large part on the retention and development of internal talent. A commitment to internal recruitment, rather than staffing higher-level positions externally, can give organizations an advantage over competitors by enabling succession planning and minimizing the risk of critical positions in the organization remaining vacant after the departure of an incumbent. Succession management practices help to ensure that successors are developed and ready to assume their new roles when an opening arises. By facilitating the smooth transitioning of talent as people move through the organization and optimally deploying talent across the organization, succession management and internal recruiting help an organization execute its business strategy and meet its business goals. Career planning is best done in conjunction with succession management to ensure that employees desire the job and career opportunities that the organization would like them to pursue.

Endnotes

[1] See Phillips, J.M. & Gully, S.M. *Strategic Staffing*, 2009. Upper Saddle River, NJ: Prentice Hall.

[2] For a more extensive discussion see Kristof-Brown, A.L., Zimmerman, R.D., and Johnson, E.C., "Consequences of Individuals' Fit at Work: A meta-analysis of person-job, person-organization, person-group, and person-supervisor fit," *Personnel Psychology*, 2005, 58, 281-342.

[3] Adapted from Edwards, J.R., "Person-job Fit: A Conceptual Integration, Literature Review, and Methodological Critique," In C.L. Cooper and I.T. Robertson (eds.), *International Review of Industrial and Organizational Psychology*, (Vol. 6), 1991, 283-357. New York: Wiley.

[4] Caldwell, D.F. & O'Reilly, C.A., "Measuring Person-job Fit Within a Profile Comparison Process," *Journal of Applied Psychology*, 1990, 75, 648-657; Edwards, J.R., "Person-job Fit: A Conceptual Integration, Literature Review, and Methodological Critique," In C.L. Cooper and I.T. Robertson (eds.), *International Review of Industrial and Organizational Psychology*, (Vol. 6), 1991, 283-357. New York: Wiley.

[5] Delaney, K.J., "Google Adjusts Hiring Process as Needs Grow," *The Wall Street Journal*, October 23, 2006, p. B1.

[6] Kristof-Brown, et al, 2005.

[7] Jacobs, R., Hofmann, D.A., & Kriska, D., "Performance and Seniority," *Human Performance*, 1990, 3(2), 107-121; Quinones, M.A., Ford, J.K., & Teachout, M.S., "The Relationship Between Work Experience and Job Performance: A Conceptual and Meta-analytic Review," *Personnel Psychology*, 1995, 48(4), pp. 887-910.

[8] Kristof-Brown, et al, 2005.

[9] Werbel, J.D. & Gilliland, S.W., "Person-environment Fit in the Selection Process," In G.R. Ferris (ed.), *Research in Personnel and Human Resource Management*, Vol. 17, 1999, 209-243. Stamford, CT: JAI Press.

[10] Peter Sinton, "Teamwork the Name of the Game for Ideo," *San Francisco Chronicle*, February 23, 2000, available online at: www.sfgate.com/cgi-bin/article.cgi?file=/chronicle/archive/2000/02/23/BU39355.DTL.

[11] Kristof, A.L., "Person-organization Fit: An Integrative Review of its Conceptualizations, Measurement, and Implications," *Personnel Psychology*, 1996, 49, 1-50; Kristof, A.L., "Perceived Applicant Fit: Distinguishing Between Recruiters' Perceptions of Person-job and Person-organization Fit," *Personnel Psychology*, 2000, 53, 643-671.

[12] E.g., Chatman, J., "Improving Interactional Organizational Research: A Model of Person-organization Fit," *Academy of Management Review*, 1989, 14, 333-349; Chatman, J., "Matching People and Organizations: Selection and Socialization in Public Accounting Firms," *Administrative Science Quarterly*, 1991, 36, 459-484;

Vancouver, J.B., & Schmitt. N.W., "An Exploratory Examination of Person-organization Fit: Organizational Goal Congruence," *Personnel Psychology*, 1991, 44, 333-52.

13 Kristof-Brown, et al, 2005.

14 Ibid.

15 O'Reilly, C.A. III, Chatman, J., & Caldwell, D.V., "People and Organizational Culture: A Profile Comparison Approach to Assessing Person-organization Fit," *Academy of Management Journal*, 1991, 34, 487-516.

16 Ashford, S.J. & Taylor, M.S., "Adaptations to Work Transitions: An Integrative Approach," In G. Ferris & K. Rowland (eds.) *Research in Personnel and Human Resources Management*, 1990, vol. 8, pp. 1-39.

17 Available online at: www.jnj.com.

18 Michaels, L., "The HR Side of Competitive Advantage," *Thunderbird Magazine*, 2002, 55 (1).

19 Holland, J.L., *Making Vocational Choices: A Theory of Vocation Personalities and Work Environments*, 1985, Englewood Cliffs, NJ: Prentice-Hall.

20 Muchinsky, P.M. & Monahan, C.J., "What is Person-environment Congruence? Supplementary Versus Complementary Models of Fit," *Journal of Vocational Behavior*, 1987, 31, 268-77.

21 Muchinsky & Monahan, 1987, 269.

22 Anders, G., "Talent Bank," *Fast Company*, June 2000, p. 94.

23 Muchinsky & Monahan, 1987, 269.

24 Boyle, M., "Why Costco is so Addictive," *Fortune*, October 25, 2006, available online at:money.cnn.com/magazines/fortune/fortune_archive/2006/10/30/8391725/index.htm?postversion=2006102515. Accessed January 16, 2009.

25 Newman, E., "Improving the Internal Recruiting Process: A Strategic Opportunity for HR," *Electronic Recruiting Exchange*, March 29, 2005, available online at: www.ere.net/articles/db/6689570981974CD49F570CC50B92DA41.asp. Accessed January 8, 2009.

26 Tyler, K., "Put Applicants' Skills To the Test," *HR Magazine*, January 2000, pp. 75-77.

27 "2007 Training Top 125," *Training Magazine*, March 2007, available online at: www.trainingmag.com/managesmarter/images/pdfs/2007Top125.pdf. Accessed January 16, 2009.

28 *Griggs v. Duke Power Co.*, 401 U.S. 424 (1971).

29 *Roberts v. Texaco, Inc.*, 94 Civ. 2015 (CLB).

30 *Abdallah v. Coca-Cola*, No. 1-98-cv-3679 (N.D. Ga. Feb. 5, 2001).

31 Equal Employment Opportunity Commission, "Uniform Employee Selection Guidelines Interpretation and Clarification (Questions and Answers)," available online at: www.uniformguidelines.com/questionandanswers.html. Accessed January 29, 2009.

32 Uniform Guideline 14C(4), 43 Fed. Reg. 38, 302 (1978).

33 Hansen, F., "Recruiting on the Right Side of the Law," *Workforce Management Online*, May 2006. Available online at: www.workforce.com/section/06/feature/24/38/12/. Accessed June 30, 2006.

34 Ibid.

35 Bergeron, C., "Build a Talent Strategy to Achieve Your Desired Business Results," *Handbook of Business Strategy*, 2004, 5(1), pp. 133-140.

36 Bechet, T.P. & Walker, L.W., "Aligning Staffing With Business Strategy," *Human Resource Planning*, 1993, 16, pp. 1-16.

37 Harris, P., "Case Study: Web-based Development Delivers for FedEx," *Learning Circuits*, September 2004, available online at: www.learningcircuits.org/2004/sep2004/harris.htm. Accessed October 31, 2007.

38 "Creating Leadership Capabilities for Success within a Rapidly Evolving Industry," Personnel Decisions International, available online at: www.personneldecisions.com/success_stories_detail.aspx?id=1138. Accessed October 16, 2007.

39 Bechet & Walker, 1993, pp. 1-16.

40 Ibid.

41 Inter-Agency Benchmarking and Best Practices Council, *Serving the American Public: Best Practices in Downsizing*, September 1997, available online at: http://gov-info.library.unt.edu/npr/library/papers/benchmrk/downsize.html#section_4. Accessed January 12, 2009.

42 Personnel Decisions International, "Aligning Talent with Changing Business Needs," available online at: www.personneldecisions.com/results/casestudydetail-generic.asp?id=24. Accessed October 16, 2007.

43 Kim, S., "Linking Employee Assessments to Succession Planning," *Public Personnel Management*, Winter 2003, 32(4): 533-48

44 McCafferty, J., "A Human Inventory," *CFO Magazine*, April 1, 2005, available online at: www.cfo.com/article.cfm/3804634/c_3805512?f=singlepage. Accessed January 16, 2009.

45 Treasury Board of Canada Secretariat, *Employee Skills Inventories for the Federal Public Service*, 1994, available online at: www.tbs-sct.gc.ca/pubs_pol/hrpubs/TB_85A/dwnld/invent_e.rtf. Accessed May 16, 2008.

46 Healy, C.C. & Welchert, A.J., "Mentoring Relations: A Definition to Advance Research and Practice," *Educational Researcher*, 19(9), p. 17.

47 Scandura, T.A., "Mentorship and Career Mobility: An Empirical Investigation," *Journal of Organizational Behavior*, 1992, 13(2), 169-74.

48 "2007 Training Top 125," *Training Magazine*, March 2007, available online at: www.trainingmag.com/managesmarter/images/pdfs/2007Top125.pdf. Accessed January 16, 2009.

49 National Academy of Public Administration. Paths to Leadership: Executive Succession Planning in the Federal Government. 1997. Washington, D.C.: National Academy of Public Administration.

50 Metzler, J.C., "Planning For Transition," American Institute of Certified Public Accountants, August 2005, Vol. 7, available online at: pcps.aicpa.org/NR/rdonlyres/42B0698A-4576-4795-AEDC-DD7E3DF5E94B/0/SFCvolume7final.pdf. Accessed January 11, 2009.

51 Pope, B., *Workforce Management: How Today's Companies Are Meeting Business and Employee Needs,* 1992, Homewood, III: Business One Irwin.

52 Dye, C.F., "Is Anyone Next in Line? Succession Plans are Critical to Ensuring a Smooth Transition When an Organization Faces an Unexpected—Or an Expected—Leadership Vacancy," *Healthcare Financial Management*, February 2005, available online at: findarticles.com/p/articles/mi_m3257/is_2_59/ai_n9772397. Accessed January 16, 2009.

53 Clark, H., "To Tell or Not to Tell," *Forbes*, October 18, 2006, available online at: www.forbes.com/2006/10/18/leadership-health-cancer-lead-manage-cx_hc_1018succession.html. Accessed January 9, 2009.

54 Charan, R., Drotter, S., & Noel, J., *The Leadership Pipeline*, 2001, San Francisco, CA: Jossey-Bass.

55 Aitchinson, C., "Succession Planning at the Dixons Group," *Strategic HR Review*, August 2004, 3(5), pp. 24-7.

56 Fulmer, R.M., "Choose Tomorrow's Leaders Today," *Graziado Business Report*, Winter 2002, available online at: gbr.pepperdine.edu/021/succession.html. Accessed January 16, 2009.

57 See Beeson, J., "Succession Planning," *Across the Board*, 2000, 37(2), pp. 38-43; Crockett, J., "Diversity: Winning Competitive Advantage Through a Diverse Workforce," *HR Focus*, 1999, 76(5), pp. 9-10; Stewart, J. K., "Diversity Efforts Dragging Women of Color Find Progress Can Be Made, But It's Slow," *Chicago Tribune*, September 1, 1999, p. 7.

58 Crockett, J., 1999, pp. 9-10; Stewart, J.K., 1999.

59 Feeney, S.A., "Irreplaceable You," *Workforce Management*, August 2003, pp. 36-40.

60 Kiger, P.J., "Succession Planning Keeps WellPoint Competitive," *Workforce*, April 2002, pp. 50-4.

61 Frauenheim, E., "Software Products Aim to Streamline Succession Planning," *Workforce Management Online*, January 2006, Available online at: www.workforce.com/section/06/feature/24/24/94/242496.html. Accessed October 13, 2006.

62 Kiger, P.J., April 2002, pp. 50-4.

63 Ibid.

64 Frauenheim, E., "Succession Progression," *Workforce Management*, January 16, 2006, pp. 31-4.

65 Charan, R., Drotter, S., & Noel, J., *The Leadership Pipeline: How to Build the Leadership-powered Company*, 2001, San Francisco, CA: Jossey-Bass, p. 167.

66 In Kesler, G.C., "Why the Leadership Bench Never Gets Deeper: Ten Insights About Executive Talent Development," *HR Planning Society Journal*, 2002, 25(1), pp. 32-44.

67 Wells, S.J., "Who's Next?" *HR Magazine*, November 2003, pp. 45-50.

68 Frauenheim, E., "Firms Walk Fine Line With 'High-Potential' Programs," *Workforce Management*, November 15, 2006, available online at: www.workforce.com/section/11/feature/24/54/84/index.html. Accessed January 6, 2009.

69 Feeny, S. (2003).

70 Guthridge, M., Komm, A.B., & Lawson, E., "The People Problem in Talent Management," *The McKinsey Quarterly*, October 26, 2006, available online at: www.mckinseyquarterly.com/article_page.aspx?ar=1755&L2=18&L3=31&srid=63&gp=1. Accessed January 5, 2009.

71 For a more thorough discussion of performance appraisal see Murphy, K.R. & Cleveland, J., *Understanding Performance Appraisal: Social, Organizational, and Goal-based Perspectives*, 1995, Thousand Oaks, CA: Sage.

72 Bernardin, H.J. & Beatty, R.W., *Performance Appraisal: Assessing Human Behavior at Work*, 1984, Boston: Kent.

73 Kiger, P.J., "Elements of WellPoint's Succession-Planning Program," *Workforce*, April 2002, p. 51.

74 Kane, J.S. & Lawler, E.E., "Performance Appraisal Effectiveness: Its Assessment and Determinants," In B. Staw (ed.), *Research in Organizational Behavior*, 1979, Vol. 1, Greenwich, CT: JAI Press.

75 Yammarino, F. & Atwater, L., "Understanding Self-perception Accuracy: Implications for Human Resource Management," *Human Resource Management*, 1993, 32(2), pp. 231-47; John, O.P. & Robins, R.W., "Accuracy and Bias in Self-Perception: Individual Differences in Self-Enhancement and the Role of Narcissism," *Journal of Personality and Social Psychology*, January 1994, 66(1), pp. 206-19; Furnham, A. & Stringfield, P., "Congruence in Job-Performance Ratings: A Study of 360 Feedback Examining Self, Manager, Peers, and Consultant Ratings," *Human Relations*, April 1998, 51(4), pp. 517-30.

76 Kingstrom, P.O. & Mainstone, L.E., "An Investigation of Rater-Ratee Acquaintance and Rater Bias," *Academy of Management Journal*, 1985, 28, pp. 641-53.

77 Borman, W.C., "The Rating of Individuals in Organizations: An Alternative Approach," *Organizational Behavior and Human Performance*, 1974, 12, pp. 105-24.

78 Reilly, R.R. & Chao, G.T., "Validity and Fairness of Some Alternative Employee Selection Procedures," *Personnel Psychology*, 1982, 35, pp. 1-62.

79 Viswesvaran, C., Ones, D.S., & Schmidt, F.L., "Comparative Analysis of the Reliability of Job Performance Ratings," *Journal of Applied Psychology*, 1991, 6, 557-74.

80 United States Office of Personnel Management, "360-Degree Assessment: An Overview," September 1997, available online at: www.opm.gov/perform/wppdf/360asess.pdf. Accessed January 11, 2009.

81 Reilly, R.R. & Chao, G.T., 1982, pp. 1-62.

82 United States Office of Personnel Management, September 1997.

83 "2007 Training Top 125," *Training Magazine*, March 2007, available online at: www.trainingmag.com/managesmarter/images/pdfs/2007Top125.pdf. Accessed January 16, 2009.

84 "Testing Becomes Key Element of Customs' Hiring and Merit Promotion Processes," *U.S. Customs Today*, November 2000, available online at: www.cbp.gov/custoday/nov2000/tests.htm. Accessed January 11, 2009.

85 Carbonara, P., "Hire for Attitude, Train for Skill," *Fast Company*, August 1996, 4, p. 73.

86 Ryan, A.M. & Sackett, P.R., "A survey of individual assessment practices by I/O psychologists," *Personnel Psychology*, 1987, 40, pp. 455-88.

87 Kleinknecht, M.K. & Hefferin, E.A., "Assisting Nurses Toward Professional Growth: A Career Development Model," *Journal of Nursing Administration*, 1982, 12(4), pp. 30-6.

88 Pope, B. (1992). *Workforce Management: How Today's Companies Are Meeting Business and Employee Needs*, Homewood, III: Business One Irwin.

89 Kimberly-Clark, "Experienced/MBAs," 2009, available online at: www.kimberly-clark.com/careers/na/exp_mba.aspx. Accessed January 16, 2009.

90 "Career Development in Canada," generalmills.com, available online at: www.generalmills.com/corporate/careers/development_canada.aspx. Accessed January 16, 2009.

91 "2007 Training Top 125," *Training Magazine*, March 2007, available online at: www.trainingmag.com/managesmarter/images/pdfs/2007Top125.pdf. Accessed January 10, 2009.

92 Gaugler, B.B., Rosenthal, D.B., Thornton, G.C. III, & Bentson, C., "Meta-analysis of Assessment Center Validity," *Journal of Applied Psychology*, 1987, 72, 493-511.

93 Brutus, S., Ruderman, M.N., Ohlott, P.J., & McCauley, C.D., "Developing from Job Experiences: The Role of Organization-based Self-esteem," *Human Resource Development Quarterly*, 2001, 11 (4), 367-80.

94 Chambers, E.G., Foulon, M., Handfield-Jones, H., Hankin, S.M., & Michaels, E.G. III, "The War for Talent," *The McKinsey Quarterly*, 1998, 3, 44-57.

95 Joinson, C., "Employee, Sculpt Thyself … With a Little Help," *HR Magazine*, May 2001, available online at: findarticles.com/p/articles/mi_m3495/is_5_46/ai_74829358/pg_2. Accessed January 6, 2009.

96 Caudron, S., "Plan Today for an Unexpected Tomorrow," *Personnel Journal*, September 1996, 75 (9), 40-5.

97 Ellis, K. (2003). Making Waves. *Training*, June 16-21.

98 Ibid.

99 Knudson, L., "Generating Leaders GE Style," 2007, *HR Management*, available online at: www.hrmreport.com/pastissue/article.asp?art=269158&issue=186. Accessed May 16, 2007.

100 For a more detailed discussion of this section's material, see Mahler, W.R. & Wrightnour, W.F., *Executive Continuity: How to Build and Retain an Effective Management Team*, 1973, Homewood, IL: Dow Jones-Irwin; Mahler, W. & Drotter, S. *The Succession Planning Handbook for the Chief Executive*, 1986, Midland Park, NJ: Mahler Publishing Co.; and Charan, R., Drotter, S., & Noel, J., *The Leadership Pipeline*, 2001, San Francisco, CA: Jossey-Bass.

101 Fulmer, R.M., "Choose Tomorrow's Leaders Today," *Graziado Business Report*, available online at: gbr.pepperdine.edu/021/succession.html. Accessed January 16, 2009.

102 Personal communication with Steve Drotter, October 13, 2006.

Index

Acknowledgments

We would like to thank our sons, Ryan and Tyler, for their support and patience while we wrote this book. We would also like to thank Pearson for allowing us to adapt some of the material from our book, *Strategic Staffing*, for use in this series. We also thank the reviewers — especially Laura Ostroff, director of Total Rewards and HRIS at Bon Secours Health System, Inc. — and the SHRM staff for this opportunity and for their suggestions and insights. If you have feedback about this book or if you would like to contact us for any reason, please e-mail us at phillipsgully@gmail.com.

About the Authors

Jean M. Phillips, Ph.D., is an associate professor of human resource management at the School of Management and Labor Relations, Rutgers University. Dr. Phillips is a current or former member of several editorial boards including *Personnel Psychology, Journal of Applied Psychology*, and *Journal of Management*. She received the 2004 Cummings Scholar Award from the Organizational Behavior Division of the Academy of Management and was among the top five percent of published authors in two of the top human resource management journals during the 1990s. She is also the co-author of the college textbooks *Managing Now!* (2007) and *Strategic Staffing* (2008) and consults in the areas of recruiting and staffing, linking employee surveys to organizational outcomes, and team effectiveness. She can be reached at phillipsgully@gmail.com.

Stanley M. Gully, Ph.D., is an associate professor of human resource management at the School of Management and Labor Relations, Rutgers University. He is a current or former member of the editorial boards of *Academy of Management Journal, Journal of Applied Psychology, Journal of Organizational Behavior*, and *Journal of Management*. He received multiple awards for his teaching, research, and service, including a research award from the American Society for Training & Development. His paper on general self-efficacy is in the top 10 most read papers in *Organizational Research Methods* and his meta-analysis on cohesion is in the top 3 most cited papers in *Small Group Research*. He is the co-author of *Strategic Staffing* (2008) and consults in the areas of recruiting and staffing, employee engagement, team effectiveness, and organizational learning interventions. He can be reached at phillipsgully@gmail.com.

Additional SHRM-Published Books

The Cultural Fit Factor: Creating an Employment Brand that Attracts, Retains, and Repels the Right Employees
By Lizz Pellet

The Employer's Immigration Compliance Desk Reference
By Gregory H. Siskind

Employment Termination Source Book
By Wendy Bliss and Gene Thornton

The Essential Guide to Workplace Investigations: How to Handle Employee Complaints & Problems
By Lisa Guerin

Hiring Source Book
By Catherine D. Fyock

Hiring Success: The Art and Science of Staffing Assessment and Employee Selection
By Steven Hunt

Human Resource Essentials: Your Guide to Starting and Running the HR Function
By Lin Grensing-Pophal

Leading With Your Heart: Diversity and Ganas for Inspired Inclusion
By Cari M. Dominguez and Jude A. Sotherlund

Outsourcing Human Resources Functions: How, Why, When, and When Not to Contract for HR Services, 2d ed.
By Mary F. Cook and Scott B. Gildner

Smart Policies for Workplace Technologies: Email, Blogs, Cell Phones and More
By Lisa Guerin

Stop Bullying at Work: Strategies and Tools for HR and Legal Professionals
By Teresa A. Daniel

Strategic Staffing: A Comprehensive System for Effective Workforce Planning, 2nd ed.
By Thomas P. Bechet

For these and other SHRM-published books, please visit www.shrm.org/publications/books/pages/default.aspx.